MW01537916

This Sashiko Embroidery Patterns Design Workbook Belongs To

____

Made in the USA
Las Vegas, NV
10 August 2021

27925384R00057